M000276576

The Leadership Journal
Second Edition

WorkMatters®

Copyright © 2018 WorkMatters, Inc., All rights reserved. No portion of this book may be reproduced mechanically, electronically, or by any other means, including photocopying, without written permission of the publisher.

ISBN-13: 978-0-9789678-6-4

WorkMatters, Inc.
P.O. Box 130756
Birmingham, AL 35213 USA

205-879-8494
gayle@workmatters.com
WorkMatters.com

I DEDICATE THIS WORKMATTERS LEADERSHIP JOURNAL TO MY CLIENTS,

whose commitment to their own goals inspired me to create a Second Edition of this Journal.

I am grateful for their trust in me, and for the opportunity to be a part of their leadership journey as they achieve what's most important to them.

Thank you!

© 2018 WorkMatters, Inc.

Life is either a daring adventure
or nothing.

~ Helen Keller

Your leadership journey is a daring adventure.

I hope by capturing your thoughts in this Leadership Journal,
you will lift up, move forward and inspire change in yourself…and others.

© 2018 WorkMatters, Inc.

Welcome to The WorkMatters Leadership Journal – Second Edition!

If you have already completed the original WorkMatters Leadership Journal, you'll find that the format in this edition is essentially the same.

Based on the positive feedback received, many people appreciate the quick weekly opportunity to reflect and focus.

People also like the simplicity of the questions or prompts. I suggest you be as specific as possible with your responses. Your responses will be more meaningful and useful to you.

The questions are intentionally created to help you identify what's working and what you appreciate. There is power in keeping a positive mindset.

You get more of what you focus on. That's why this "focusing tool" is instrumental to help you stay positive—to note your thoughts, strengthen your leadership and direct your actions throughout the year.

Some leaders have had great success sharing their weekly entries with their teams or a trusted colleague. Others enjoy capturing their own thoughts privately to gain the personal clarity and focus they need.

Do what works for you.

You'll find a variety of my favorite inspirational quotes that are especially relevant to leaders like you who want to make a difference. They are designed to lift your spirits, push you forward and help you inspire the change you want.

© 2018 WorkMatters, Inc.

About Gayle Lantz

Gayle Lantz is a leadership expert and founder of **WorkMatters, Inc.,** (www.WorkMatters.com) a consulting firm dedicated to helping leaders think and work smarter.

A sought-after consultant, executive coach, facilitator, and speaker, Gayle works closely with executives and leadership teams to expand their vision, think and act strategically, and inspire change. Together, they increase business results and help make work matter at every level of the organization. Among her clients are NASA, Microsoft, MassMutual, Southern Company, Lockheed Martin, BBVA Compass Bank as well as a variety of small and mid-sized professional service firms.

Gayle runs senior executive roundtable groups comprised of executives from non-competing industries. Participants meet regularly to exchange ideas, sharpen executive leadership skills and gain objective perspective to help them grow their business.

Gayle is author of the award-winning book *Take the Bull by the Horns: The Busy Leader's Action Guide to Growing Your Business...and Yourself.*

Before starting her own business, Gayle worked as an executive in the insurance, financial services and investment industry. She most recently held an officer level position with TIAA-CREF -- a leader in its industry serving those in the academic, medical, cultural and research fields.

Gayle's articles and/or quotes have been featured in a variety of national and global business publications including *BusinessWeek, Harvard Management Update, Wall Street Journal Online, FastCompany.com, CEO Online and The New York Times.*

Gayle is a graduate of Emory University in Atlanta, Georgia. She lives in Birmingham, Alabama, and has been honored as one of Birmingham's Top 10 Women in Business.

CONTACT:
205-879-8494
gayle@workmatters.com
workmatters.com

© 2018 WorkMatters, Inc.

Introduction

Studies show that you are much more likely to achieve your goals just by writing them down. Most people don't.

This journal is designed to help you accomplish what's most important to you this year. It's simple. And requires just a little discipline.

You can use it to help you take needed steps on a weekly basis to achieve what you really want in your leadership role, business and/or personal life.

A few reasons to write down your goals:

You will...

1. Gain needed clarity about what's most important to you and where you want to go.

2. Sharpen your focus. When you're highly focused on what you want to accomplish, you'll be less likely to be pulled in other directions.

3. Build momentum. It's motivating to see progress—step by step.

4. Increase your accountability. It's one thing to say you want to accomplish something. When you write it down, you will be more committed.

5. Increase your sense of accomplishment. No more being busy. You'll work with greater purpose and conviction—and get more done.

6. Accelerate your progress. With a clear target, you can move forward more quickly and strategically.

7. Communicate your goals more clearly to others. When you have a consistent way to express what you're trying to accomplish, other people can better follow or support you.

8. Be more decisive. You will have a better basis for decision-making.

9. Become more disciplined by focusing on what really matters to you on a regular basis.

10. Be able to look back and celebrate success!

© 2018 WorkMatters, Inc.

So let's get started!

I'll ask you a few coaching questions along the way.
You'll also find quotes to keep you inspired.

Plan to spend 10-15 minutes each week to focus on what's most important to you.
If you get stuck or miss a week, simply get back on track. Habits take time to establish. Don't feel guilty or abandon the process. Jump back in and keep moving.

This is *your* process.
There are no grades. No judgment.
Just an opportunity to get clear and achieve what you *really* want.

Here are some questions to kick-start the process…

What's something you would be very excited to accomplish this year? In your work or in your life? Something that *you* really want? (Not what anyone else thinks you should want, what *you* really want.)

Be specific. What does it look like, feel like? Describe the scene in detail.

Why is the goal important to you?

What will it do for you or others?

How will you know you're making progress during the year? Any milestones or measures of success?

Make it BIG!

Believable. Is it something you really believe you can do?

I believe I can achieve this goal because_____.

Impactful. Is it something that will make a significant difference or impact?

The impact when I achieve this goal will be _____.

Gutsy. Does it make you a little nervous?

To overcome any nervousness or anxiety as I work toward my goal, I will

_____.

© 2018 WorkMatters, Inc.

"At the moment of commitment, the entire universe conspires to assist you."
~ *Johann Wolfgang von Goethe*

My BIG goal for the year is:

_____

_____

_____

_____

_____

Once you're clear, determine what you will do each week to achieve your goal.

You may want to map out specific steps in advance to the extent you can. Or you can take one week at a time and figure it out as you go.

No pressure. Just focus.

© 2018 WorkMatters, Inc.

A FEW TIPS TO GET THE MOST OUT OF YOUR
JOURNALING EXPERIENCE

TIP #1:

Be consistent. Spend time with your journal at the same time each week. Commit just 10 to 15 minutes. Put the commitment on your calendar

TIP #2:

Respond to each of the five prompting statements each week. They are all important.
Don't overthink. Just write.

TIP #3:

Commit to specific timeframes or deadlines to see better results.
What will you do by when? Be as specific as possible when you commit to action.

TIP #4:

Use the "Notes" section to capture whatever bubbles up as you're thinking. Consider recording your action items there. It might be an unrelated idea, a concern, a hope, an image. There's no "right way" to use the space. Use it as you wish.

TIP #5:

Talk about your goals and ideas with a friend, coach, mentor, accountability partner—someone you trust in your network or mastermind group. You'll be even more likely to achieve what you want.

****

I wish you much success as you accomplish what's most important to you this year.

Let this leadership journal be one way to provide the assistance you need.
And let me know if I can be of any help along the way.

Your work matters.

Gayle

© 2018 WorkMatters, Inc.

Additional WorkMatters Resources

1. My Blog

For additional insight to help you achieve what's most important, subscribe to my blog.

You'll find ideas and insights in posts I publish throughout the year.

Get a dose of timely inspiration as you accomplish your leadership and personal goals!

Visit: <u>www.workmatters.com/blog</u>

2. "My Daily Coach" App

If you'd like a little coaching each day, download my *free* mobile app: **My Daily Coach**

You'll receive a simple coaching message each day designed to keep you thinking and working smarter.

It's available for your smart phone or Ipad through the App Store or Google Play. Search my name to find it easily.

© 2018 WorkMatters, Inc.

3. Life Work Planning Workbook

Thinking about what you really want in your life and work? This resource is designed to make the process a little easier for you.

It's ideal if you're near or contemplating some kind of turning point in your life, work or leadership role. You'll find useful ideas, processes and tools to help you gain more clarity and achieve what's most important to you.

You'll find the **Life Work Planning Workbook** to be a nice complement to **The Leadership Journal.**

Find the Life Work Planning Workbook on Amazon.com.

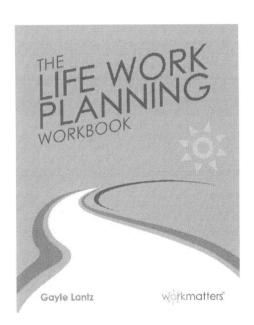

© 2018 WorkMatters, Inc.

Week 1

"Start where you are. Use what you have. Do what you can."
~ Arthur Ashe

My most important goal for this week is:

_____

_____

What I've accomplished since last week:

_____

_____

An opportunity I have or can create this week is:

_____

_____

What I've learned within the last week:

_____

_____

What I'm grateful for now:

_____

_____

© 2018 WorkMatters, Inc.

NOTES

© 2018 WorkMatters, Inc.

Week 2

"Successful people believe that they have the capability within themselves to make desirable things happen."

~ Marshall Goldsmith

My most important goal for this week is:

_____

_____

What I've accomplished since last week:

_____

_____

An opportunity I have or can create this week is:

_____

_____

What I've learned within the last week:

_____

_____

What I'm grateful for now:

_____

_____

© 2018 WorkMatters, Inc.

NOTES

© 2018 WorkMatters, Inc.

Week 3

"Before you are a leader, success is all about growing yourself. When you become a leader, success is all about growing others."
~ Jack Welch

My most important goal for this week is:

_____

_____

What I've accomplished since last week:

_____

_____

An opportunity I have or can create this week is:

_____

_____

What I've learned within the last week:

_____

_____

What I'm grateful for now:

_____

_____

© 2018 WorkMatters, Inc.

NOTES

© 2018 WorkMatters, Inc.

Week 4

"Anything's possible if you've got enough nerve."
~ *J.K. Rowling*

My most important goal for this week is:

_____

_____

What I've accomplished since last week:

_____

_____

An opportunity I have or can create this week is:

_____

_____

What I've learned within the last week:

_____

_____

What I'm grateful for now:

_____

_____

© 2018 WorkMatters, Inc.

NOTES

_____

_____

_____

_____

_____

_____

_____

_____

_____

_____

_____

_____

_____

© 2018 WorkMatters, Inc.

Week 5

"Leadership is a series of behaviors rather than a role for heroes."
~ Margaret Wheatley

My most important goal for this week is:

_____

_____

What I've accomplished since last week:

_____

_____

An opportunity I have or can create this week is:

_____

_____

What I've learned within the last week:

_____

_____

What I'm grateful for now:

_____

_____

© 2018 WorkMatters, Inc.

NOTES

© 2018 WorkMatters, Inc.

Week 6

Date: _____

"The measure of a leader is not what you do,
but what others do because of you."
~*Howard Hendricks*

My most important goal for this week is:

_____

_____

What I've accomplished since last week:

_____

_____

An opportunity I have or can create this week is:

_____

_____

What I've learned within the last week:

_____

_____

What I'm grateful for now:

_____

_____

© 2018 WorkMatters, Inc.

NOTES

© 2018 WorkMatters, Inc.

Week 7

"Train people well enough so they can leave.
Treat them well enough so they don't want to."
~ *Sir Richard Branson*

My most important goal for this week is:

_____

_____

What I've accomplished since last week:

_____

_____

An opportunity I have or can create this week is:

_____

_____

What I've learned within the last week:

_____

_____

What I'm grateful for now:

_____

_____

© 2018 WorkMatters, Inc.

NOTES

© 2018 WorkMatters, Inc.

Week 8

"The greatest glory in living lies not in never falling,
but in rising every time we fall."
~ *Nelson Mandela*

My most important goal for this week is:

_____

_____

What I've accomplished since last week:

_____

_____

An opportunity I have or can create this week is:

_____

_____

What I've learned within the last week:

_____

_____

What I'm grateful for now:

_____

_____

© 2018 WorkMatters, Inc.

NOTES

© 2018 WorkMatters, Inc.

Week 9

"Courage is what it takes to stand up and speak,
it's also what it takes to sit down and listen."
~ *Winston Churchill*

My most important goal for this week is:

_____

_____

What I've accomplished since last week:

_____

_____

An opportunity I have or can create this week is:

_____

_____

What I've learned within the last week:

_____

_____

What I'm grateful for now:

_____

_____

© 2018 WorkMatters, Inc.

NOTES

© 2018 WorkMatters, Inc.

Week 10

Date: _____

"If you don't like something change it.
If you can't change it, change the way you think about it."
~ Mary Engelbreit

My most important goal for this week is:

_____

_____

What I've accomplished since last week:

_____

_____

An opportunity I have or can create this week is:

_____

_____

What I've learned within the last week:

_____

_____

What I'm grateful for now:

_____

_____

© 2018 WorkMatters, Inc.

NOTES

_____

_____

_____

_____

_____

_____

_____

_____

_____

_____

_____

_____

_____

_____

_____

© 2018 WorkMatters, Inc.

Week 11

"Strategic leaders must not get consumed by the operational and tactical side of their work. They have a duty to find time to shape the future."
~ *Stephanie S. Mead*

My most important goal for this week is:

_____

_____

What I've accomplished since last week:

_____

_____

An opportunity I have or can create this week is:

_____

_____

What I've learned within the last week:

_____

_____

What I'm grateful for now:

_____

_____

© 2018 WorkMatters, Inc.

NOTES

© 2018 WorkMatters, Inc.

Week 12

Date: _____

"I never thought in terms of leader.
I thought very simply in terms of helping people."
~ John Hume

My most important goal for this week is:

_____

_____

What I've accomplished since last week:

_____

_____

An opportunity I have or can create this week is:

_____

_____

What I've learned within the last week:

_____

_____

What I'm grateful for now:

_____

_____

© 2018 WorkMatters, Inc.

NOTES

© 2018 WorkMatters, Inc.

Week 13

"Don't be intimidated by what you don't know. That can be your greatest strength and ensure that you do things differently from everyone else."
~ *Sara Blakely*

My most important goal for this week is:

_____

_____

What I've accomplished since last week:

_____

_____

An opportunity I have or can create this week is:

_____

_____

What I've learned within the last week:

_____

_____

What I'm grateful for now:

_____

_____

© 2018 WorkMatters, Inc.

NOTES

© 2018 WorkMatters, Inc.

Week 14

"You have to be odd to be number one."
~ Dr. Seuss

My most important goal for this week is:

_____

_____

What I've accomplished since last week:

_____

_____

An opportunity I have or can create this week is:

_____

_____

What I've learned within the last week:

_____

_____

What I'm grateful for now:

_____

_____

38

© 2018 WorkMatters, Inc.

NOTES

© 2018 WorkMatters, Inc.

Week 15

"You attract the right things when you have a sense of who you are."
~ *Amy Poehler*

My most important goal for this week is:

_____

_____

What I've accomplished since last week:

_____

_____

An opportunity I have or can create this week is:

_____

_____

What I've learned within the last week:

_____

_____

What I'm grateful for now:

_____

_____

© 2018 WorkMatters, Inc.

NOTES

© 2018 WorkMatters, Inc.

Week 16

"If you chase two rabbits, you will catch neither one."
~ *Russian Proverb*

My most important goal for this week is:

_____

_____

What I've accomplished since last week:

_____

_____

An opportunity I have or can create this week is:

_____

_____

What I've learned within the last week:

_____

_____

What I'm grateful for now:

_____

_____

© 2018 WorkMatters, Inc.

NOTES

© 2018 WorkMatters, Inc.

Week 17

"They always say time changes things,
but you actually have to change them yourself."
~ *Andy Warhol*

My most important goal for this week is:

_____

_____

What I've accomplished since last week:

_____

_____

An opportunity I have or can create this week is:

_____

_____

What I've learned within the last week:

_____

_____

What I'm grateful for now:

_____

_____

© 2018 WorkMatters, Inc.

NOTES

© 2018 WorkMatters, Inc.

Week 18

"The hardest thing to learn in life is knowing which bridge to cross and which to burn."

~ *David Russell*

My most important goal for this week is:

_____

_____

What I've accomplished since last week:

_____

_____

An opportunity I have or can create this week is:

_____

_____

What I've learned within the last week:

_____

_____

What I'm grateful for now:

_____

_____

© 2018 WorkMatters, Inc.

NOTES

© 2018 WorkMatters, Inc.

Week 19

"Management is doing things right. Leadership is doing the right things."
~ Peter Drucker

My most important goal for this week is:

_____

_____

What I've accomplished since last week:

_____

_____

An opportunity I have or can create this week is:

_____

_____

What I've learned within the last week:

_____

_____

What I'm grateful for now:

_____

_____

© 2018 WorkMatters, Inc.

NOTES

© 2018 WorkMatters, Inc.

Week 20

"There is just one thing that makes your dream impossible:
the fear of failure."
~ Paulo Coelho

My most important goal for this week is:

_____

_____

What I've accomplished since last week:

_____

_____

An opportunity I have or can create this week is:

_____

_____

What I've learned within the last week:

_____

_____

What I'm grateful for now:

_____

_____

© 2018 WorkMatters, Inc.

NOTES

© 2018 WorkMatters, Inc.

Week 21

"You need to learn how to select your thoughts just the same way you select your clothes every day. This is a power you can cultivate."
~ Elizabeth Gilbert

My most important goal for this week is:

_____

_____

What I've accomplished since last week:

_____

_____

An opportunity I have or can create this week is:

_____

_____

What I've learned within the last week:

_____

_____

What I'm grateful for now:

_____

_____

© 2018 WorkMatters, Inc.

NOTES

© 2018 WorkMatters, Inc.

Week 22

*"The problem with being a leader is that you're never sure
if you're being followed or chased."*
~ *Claire A. Murray*

My most important goal for this week is:

_____

_____

What I've accomplished since last week:

_____

_____

An opportunity I have or can create this week is:

_____

_____

What I've learned within the last week:

_____

_____

What I'm grateful for now:

_____

_____

© 2018 WorkMatters, Inc.

NOTES

© 2018 WorkMatters, Inc.

Week 23

Date: _____

"Where you stumble and fall, there you will find gold."
~ Joseph Campbell

My most important goal for this week is:

_____

_____

What I've accomplished since last week:

_____

_____

An opportunity I have or can create this week is:

_____

_____

What I've learned within the last week:

_____

_____

What I'm grateful for now:

_____

_____

© 2018 WorkMatters, Inc.

NOTES

© 2018 WorkMatters, Inc.

Week 24

Date: _____

"Even if you're on the right track, you'll get run over if you sit there."
~ *Will Rogers*

My most important goal for this week is:

_____

_____

What I've accomplished since last week:

_____

_____

An opportunity I have or can create this week is:

_____

_____

What I've learned within the last week:

_____

_____

What I'm grateful for now:

_____

_____

58

© 2018 WorkMatters, Inc.

NOTES

© 2018 WorkMatters, Inc.

Week 25

"First rule of leadership: Everything is your fault."
~ A Bug's Life

My most important goal for this week is:

_____

_____

What I've accomplished since last week:

_____

_____

An opportunity I have or can create this week is:

_____

_____

What I've learned within the last week:

_____

_____

What I'm grateful for now:

_____

_____

60

NOTES

© 2018 WorkMatters, Inc.

Week 26

"The most difficult thing is the decision to act, the rest is merely tenacity."
~ Amelia Earhart

My most important goal for this week is:

_____

_____

What I've accomplished since last week:

_____

_____

An opportunity I have or can create this week is:

_____

_____

What I've learned within the last week:

_____

_____

What I'm grateful for now:

_____

_____

© 2018 WorkMatters, Inc.

NOTES

© 2018 WorkMatters, Inc.

Week 27

*"If you want to succeed, you should strike out on new paths,
rather than travel the worn paths of accepted success."*
~ John Rockefeller

My most important goal for this week is:

_____

_____

What I've accomplished since last week:

_____

_____

An opportunity I have or can create this week is:

_____

_____

What I've learned within the last week:

_____

_____

What I'm grateful for now:

_____

_____

© 2018 WorkMatters, Inc.

NOTES

© 2018 WorkMatters, Inc.

Week 28

"You can waste your life drawing lines.
Or you can live your life crossing them."
~ Shonda Rhimes

My most important goal for this week is:

_____

_____

What I've accomplished since last week:

_____

_____

An opportunity I have or can create this week is:

_____

_____

What I've learned within the last week:

_____

_____

What I'm grateful for now:

_____

_____

© 2018 WorkMatters, Inc.

NOTES

© 2018 WorkMatters, Inc.

Week 29

Date: _____

"The question isn't who is going to let me; it's who is going to stop me."
~ Ayn Rand

My most important goal for this week is:

_____

_____

What I've accomplished since last week:

_____

_____

An opportunity I have or can create this week is:

_____

_____

What I've learned within the last week:

_____

_____

What I'm grateful for now:

_____

_____

© 2018 WorkMatters, Inc.

NOTES

© 2018 WorkMatters, Inc.

Week 30

"You can't be that kid standing at the top of the waterslide, overthinking it. You have to go down the chute."
~ *Tina Fey*

My most important goal for this week is:

_____

_____

What I've accomplished since last week:

_____

_____

An opportunity I have or can create this week is:

_____

_____

What I've learned within the last week:

_____

_____

What I'm grateful for now:

_____

_____

© 2018 WorkMatters, Inc.

NOTES

_____

_____

_____

_____

_____

_____

_____

_____

_____

_____

_____

_____

_____

_____

© 2018 WorkMatters, Inc.

Week 31

"If you just work on stuff that you like and do what you're passionate about, you don't have to have a master plan with how things will play out."
~ Mark Zuckerberg

My most important goal for this week is:

_____

_____

What I've accomplished since last week:

_____

_____

An opportunity I have or can create this week is:

_____

_____

What I've learned within the last week:

_____

_____

What I'm grateful for now:

_____

_____

© 2018 WorkMatters, Inc.

NOTES

© 2018 WorkMatters, Inc.

Week 32

"Real courage is when you know you're licked before you begin,
but you begin anyway and see it through no matter what."
~ *Harper Lee*

My most important goal for this week is:

_____

_____

What I've accomplished since last week:

_____

_____

An opportunity I have or can create this week is:

_____

_____

What I've learned within the last week:

_____

_____

What I'm grateful for now:

_____

_____

© 2018 WorkMatters, Inc.

NOTES

© 2018 WorkMatters, Inc.

Week 33

"The best time to plant a tree was 20 years ago.
The second-best time is now."
~ *Chinese Proverb*

My most important goal for this week is:

_____

_____

What I've accomplished since last week:

_____

_____

An opportunity I have or can create this week is:

_____

_____

What I've learned within the last week:

_____

_____

What I'm grateful for now:

_____

_____

© 2018 WorkMatters, Inc.

NOTES

© 2018 WorkMatters, Inc.

Week 34

"Ideas are easy. Implementation is hard."
~ *Guy Kawasaki*

My most important goal for this week is:

_____

_____

What I've accomplished since last week:

_____

_____

An opportunity I have or can create this week is:

_____

_____

What I've learned within the last week:

_____

_____

What I'm grateful for now:

_____

_____

© 2018 WorkMatters, Inc.

NOTES

_____

_____

_____

_____

_____

_____

_____

_____

_____

_____

_____

_____

_____

_____

© 2018 WorkMatters, Inc.

Week 35

"A person who never made a mistake never tried anything new."
~ Albert Einstein

My most important goal for this week is:

_____

_____

What I've accomplished since last week:

_____

_____

An opportunity I have or can create this week is:

_____

_____

What I've learned within the last week:

_____

_____

What I'm grateful for now:

_____

_____

80

© 2018 WorkMatters, Inc.

NOTES

© 2018 WorkMatters, Inc.

Week 36

"Leaders think and talk about the solutions.
Followers think and talk about the problems."
~ Brian Tracey

My most important goal for this week is:

_____

_____

What I've accomplished since last week:

_____

_____

An opportunity I have or can create this week is:

_____

_____

What I've learned within the last week:

_____

_____

What I'm grateful for now:

_____

_____

© 2018 WorkMatters, Inc.

NOTES

© 2018 WorkMatters, Inc.

Week 37

*"To be a good leader, you cannot major in the minor things,
and you must be less distracted than your competition."*
~ *Tim Ferris*

My most important goal for this week is:

_____

_____

What I've accomplished since last week:

_____

_____

An opportunity I have or can create this week is:

_____

_____

What I've learned within the last week:

_____

_____

What I'm grateful for now:

_____

_____

© 2018 WorkMatters, Inc.

NOTES

© 2018 WorkMatters, Inc.

Week 38

"The truth is, leaders need to keep an open mind while being flexible, and adjust as necessary."
~ Daymond John

My most important goal for this week is:

_____

_____

What I've accomplished since last week:

_____

_____

An opportunity I have or can create this week is:

_____

_____

What I've learned within the last week:

_____

_____

What I'm grateful for now:

_____

_____

© 2018 WorkMatters, Inc.

NOTES

© 2018 WorkMatters, Inc.

Week 39

"You will get all you want in life,
if you help enough other people get what they want."
~ *Zig Ziglar*

My most important goal for this week is:

_____

_____

What I've accomplished since last week:

_____

_____

An opportunity I have or can create this week is:

_____

_____

What I've learned within the last week:

_____

_____

What I'm grateful for now:

_____

_____

© 2018 WorkMatters, Inc.

NOTES

© 2018 WorkMatters, Inc.

Week 40

"The secret to leadership is simple: Do what you believe in.
Paint a picture of the future. Go there. People will follow."
~ Seth Godin

My most important goal for this week is:

_____

_____

What I've accomplished since last week:

_____

_____

An opportunity I have or can create this week is:

_____

_____

What I've learned within the last week:

_____

_____

What I'm grateful for now:

_____

_____

© 2018 WorkMatters, Inc.

NOTES

_____

_____

_____

_____

_____

_____

_____

_____

_____

_____

_____

_____

_____

_____

© 2018 WorkMatters, Inc.

Week 41

"Anyone can hold the helm when the sea is calm."
~ *Publilius Syrus*

My most important goal for this week is:

_____

_____

What I've accomplished since last week:

_____

_____

An opportunity I have or can create this week is:

_____

_____

What I've learned within the last week:

_____

_____

What I'm grateful for now:

_____

_____

© 2018 WorkMatters, Inc.

NOTES

© 2018 WorkMatters, Inc.

Week 42

"The only limit to your impact is your imagination and commitment."
~ *Tony Robbins*

My most important goal for this week is:

_____

_____

What I've accomplished since last week:

_____

_____

An opportunity I have or can create this week is:

_____

_____

What I've learned within the last week:

_____

_____

What I'm grateful for now:

_____

_____

© 2018 WorkMatters, Inc.

NOTES

© 2018 WorkMatters, Inc.

Week 43

Date: _____

"Fear, to a great extent, is born of a story we tell ourselves."
~ *Cheryl Strayed*

My most important goal for this week is:

_____

_____

What I've accomplished since last week:

_____

_____

An opportunity I have or can create this week is:

_____

_____

What I've learned within the last week:

_____

_____

What I'm grateful for now:

_____

_____

© 2018 WorkMatters, Inc.

NOTES

© 2018 WorkMatters, Inc.

Week 44

"Our lives begin to end the day we become silent about things that matter."
~ Martin Luther King Jr.

My most important goal for this week is:

_____

_____

What I've accomplished since last week:

_____

_____

An opportunity I have or can create this week is:

_____

_____

What I've learned within the last week:

_____

_____

What I'm grateful for now:

_____

_____

© 2018 WorkMatters, Inc.

NOTES

© 2018 WorkMatters, Inc.

Week 45

"You don't inspire your teammates by showing them how great you are.
You inspire them by showing them how great they are."
~ *Robyn Benincasa*

My most important goal for this week is:

_____

_____

What I've accomplished since last week:

_____

_____

An opportunity I have or can create this week is:

_____

_____

What I've learned within the last week:

_____

_____

What I'm grateful for now:

_____

_____

© 2018 WorkMatters, Inc.

NOTES

_____

_____

_____

_____

_____

_____

_____

_____

_____

_____

_____

_____

_____

_____

_____

© 2018 WorkMatters, Inc.

Week 46

*"People at work are thirsting for context, yearning to know
that what they do contributes to a larger whole."*
~ *Daniel Pink*

My most important goal for this week is:

_____

_____

What I've accomplished since last week:

_____

_____

An opportunity I have or can create this week is:

_____

_____

What I've learned within the last week:

_____

_____

What I'm grateful for now:

_____

_____

© 2018 WorkMatters, Inc.

NOTES

© 2018 WorkMatters, Inc.

Week 47

"The essence of strategy is choosing what not to do."
~ Michael Porter

My most important goal for this week is:

_____

_____

What I've accomplished since last week:

_____

_____

An opportunity I have or can create this week is:

_____

_____

What I've learned within the last week:

_____

_____

What I'm grateful for now:

_____

_____

© 2018 WorkMatters, Inc.

NOTES

© 2018 WorkMatters, Inc.

Week 48

*"The growth and development of people is
the highest calling of leadership."*
~ *Harvey Firestone*

My most important goal for this week is:

_____

_____

What I've accomplished since last week:

_____

_____

An opportunity I have or can create this week is:

_____

_____

What I've learned within the last week:

_____

_____

What I'm grateful for now:

_____

_____

© 2018 WorkMatters, Inc.

NOTES

© 2018 WorkMatters, Inc.

Week 49

> *"Leadership is about making others better as a result of your presence and making sure that impact lasts in your absence."*
> ~ *Sheryl Sandberg*

My most important goal for this week is:

_____

_____

What I've accomplished since last week:

_____

_____

An opportunity I have or can create this week is:

_____

_____

What I've learned within the last week:

_____

_____

What I'm grateful for now:

_____

_____

© 2018 WorkMatters, Inc.

NOTES

© 2018 WorkMatters, Inc.

Week 50

"If work isn't fun, you're not playing on the right team."
~ Frank Sonnenberg

My most important goal for this week is:

_____

_____

What I've accomplished since last week:

_____

_____

An opportunity I have or can create this week is:

_____

_____

What I've learned within the last week:

_____

_____

What I'm grateful for now:

_____

_____

© 2018 WorkMatters, Inc.

NOTES

© 2018 WorkMatters, Inc.

Week 51

"You must do something heartfelt. And you must do it soon.
Let go of all this effort, and let yourself down, however awkwardly, into the
waters of the work you want."
~ David Whyte

My most important goal for this week is:

_____

_____

What I've accomplished since last week:

_____

_____

An opportunity I have or can create this week is:

_____

_____

What I've learned within the last week:

_____

_____

What I'm grateful for now:

© 2018 WorkMatters, Inc.

NOTES

© 2018 WorkMatters, Inc.

Week 52

*"Our chief want is someone who will inspire us
to be what we know we could be."*
~Ralph Waldo Emerson

My most important goal for this week is:

_____

_____

What I've accomplished since last week:

_____

_____

An opportunity I have or can create this week is:

_____

_____

What I've learned within the last week:

_____

_____

What I'm grateful for now:

_____

_____

© 2018 WorkMatters, Inc.